W9-BBP-868

ABCD

HISTORY MYSTERY

Chicago Historical Society

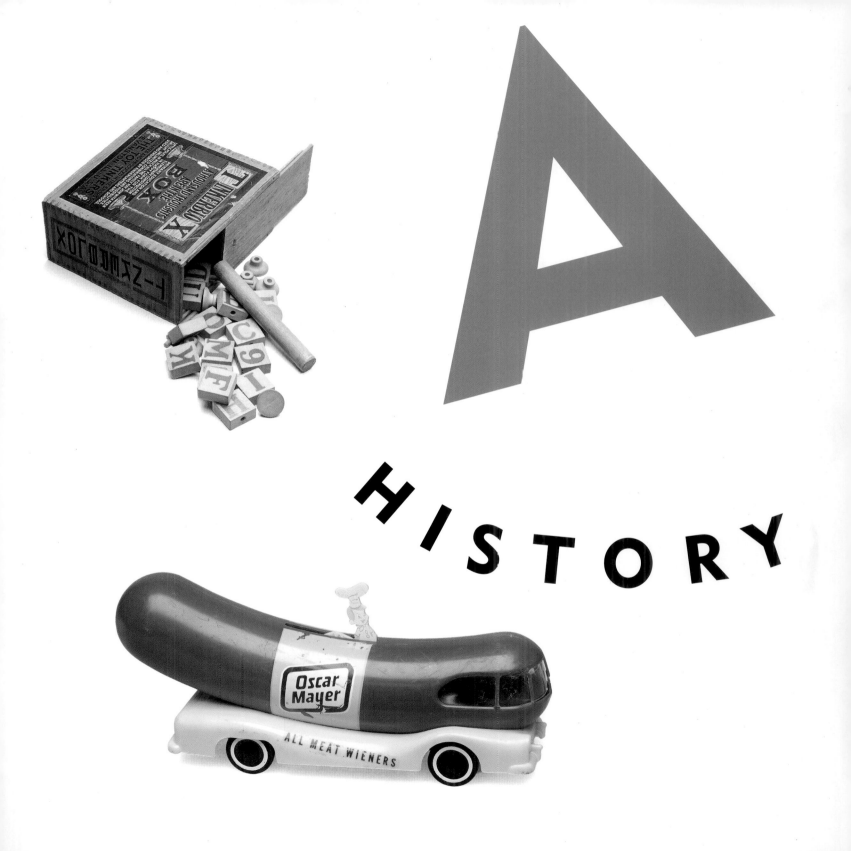

A HISTORY

B C

MYSTERY

A
CHICAGO
HISTORICAL
SOCIETY
ALPHABET

© 2000 Chicago Historical Society
Chicago Historical Society
Clark Street at North Avenue
Chicago IL 60614
www.chicagohistory.org

Produced by the Chicago Historical Society
Project Editor: Gwen Ihnat
Director of Publications: Rosemary K. Adams
Director of History Programs: D. Lynn McRainey

Designed and typeset by Joan Sommers Design, Chicago
Printed and bound by Palace Press International, China
Color separations by Professional Graphics, Rockford, Illinois

Special thanks to the Chicago Historical Society staff
   members who offered their assistance on this project:
Photography: John Alderson, Jay Crawford
Collection Services: Nancy Buenger, M. Alison Eisendrath, Julie
   Katz, Robert Kent, Timothy A. Long
Research and Access: Matt Cook, Lesley A. Martin, Leigh Moran
Exhibitions: Tamara Biggs, Stephen H. McLemore, Matthias Regan

Library of Congress Catalog Card Number: 00-108517
ISBN 0-913820-23-7

Photograph and artifact credits:

All objects come from the collection of the Chicago Historical Society.

A: Alphabet blocks, 1983.349; B: Bicycle, 1955, 1986.231; C: Camera, ICHi-29806; photograph of women with movie camera, DN-0085715; D: Doll, c. 1890, x.1149; E: Papier-mache elephant, c. 1890, 1953.18; F: Fire King number one, 1924.32; photograph of Fire King, ICHi-02657; G: Gum machine, 1991.630.2; gum wrappers, CHS collection; H: Wienermobile, c. 1965, 1992.155.1; I: Ice skates, 1982.197.1ab; photographs of skating, SDN-1076 (left) and DN-0078356 (right); J: Jukebox by Rock-ola Manufacturing Company, 1939, 1975.135; photograph of couple dancing, DN-0081644; record images by Photodisc; K: Keys, 1961.35; 920.IH; 1138-IH; no #; L: Letter, CHS manuscripts, Chicago Fire of 1871 collection; stamps, CHS manuscripts; M: Barnes-Crosby photograph of Maxwell Street market, c. 1905, ICHi-19155; fruit images by Photodisc; N: *Chicago Tribune*, November 3, 1948; photograph of champion newsboy, DN-0001815; O: Wizard of Oz poster, lithograph, by Will W. Denslow, 1900; P: Kuklapolitan puppets, 1985.549.1-79; Q: 1933 Century of Progress Exposition quilts, 1991.632 (left) and 1995.149 (right); R: Pioneer engine locomotive, 1836, 1972.42; S: Selection of shoes from the Chicago Historical Society collection; shoes worn by Michael Jordan, 1989, 1990.83a-f; T: clockwise from top left: Tootsie toys, c. 1935, 1981.256a-f; Lincoln logs, c. 1955, 1984.332.3; Midgetoys, 1983.747.3; 1983.747.4; 1983.747.11; Toy fire truck, c. 1920, 1964.942; Tinkerblox, c. 1917, 1984.332.5; U: Girl Scout leader uniform, 1948, 1985.631.1a-e; photograph of Girl Scout "cookie champ" Sidney Stratton, 1935, ICHi-20166 ; V: Valentines, CHS collection; W: clockwise from top: Celtic knot motif window by Healy & Millet, 1880s, 1985.767.1; scroll motif window by George A. Misch & Bros., c. 1890, 1984.392.1; thistle pattern window by George Maher and Louis Millet, 1901, 1985.170.2; X: Hedrich-Blessing photograph of the John Hancock Building, c. 1970, HB-31216 F3; Y: Yoke, 1941.187abc; plowing image by Deberny Type Foundry, c. 1910; Z: Zither, c. 1900, 1988.351.

This book was made possible
by the generous donation of the
Joseph L. and Emily K. Gidwitz
Memorial Foundation.

The Chicago Historical Society is adding some mystery to our history. Can you guess what these objects are before you turn the page?

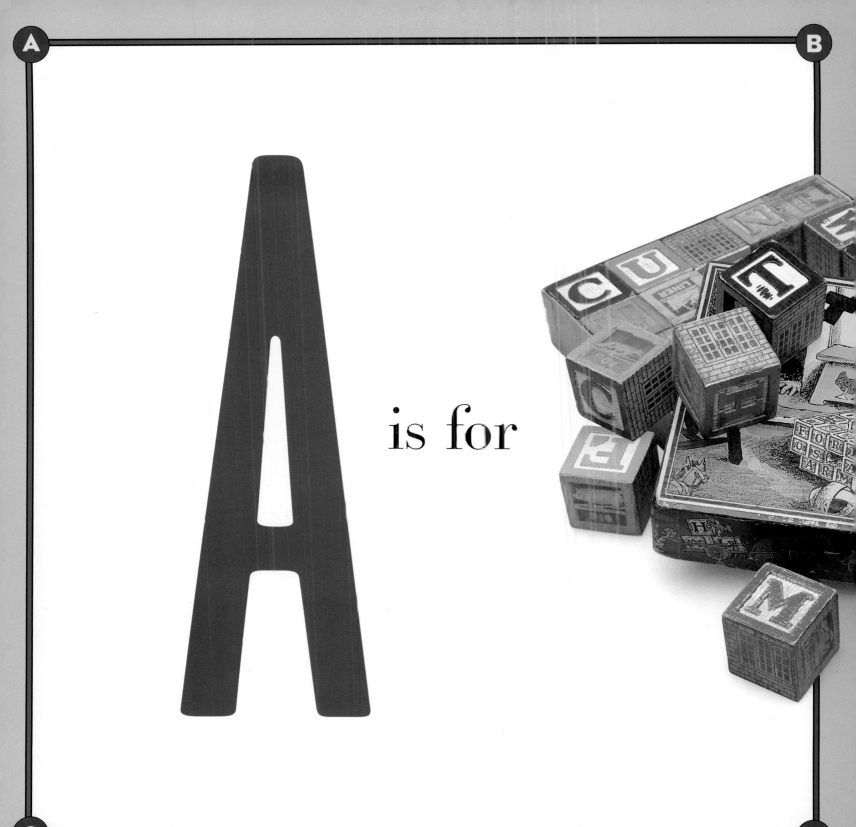

A is for

Alphabet blocks

Bicycle

C is for

Camera

D is for

Doll

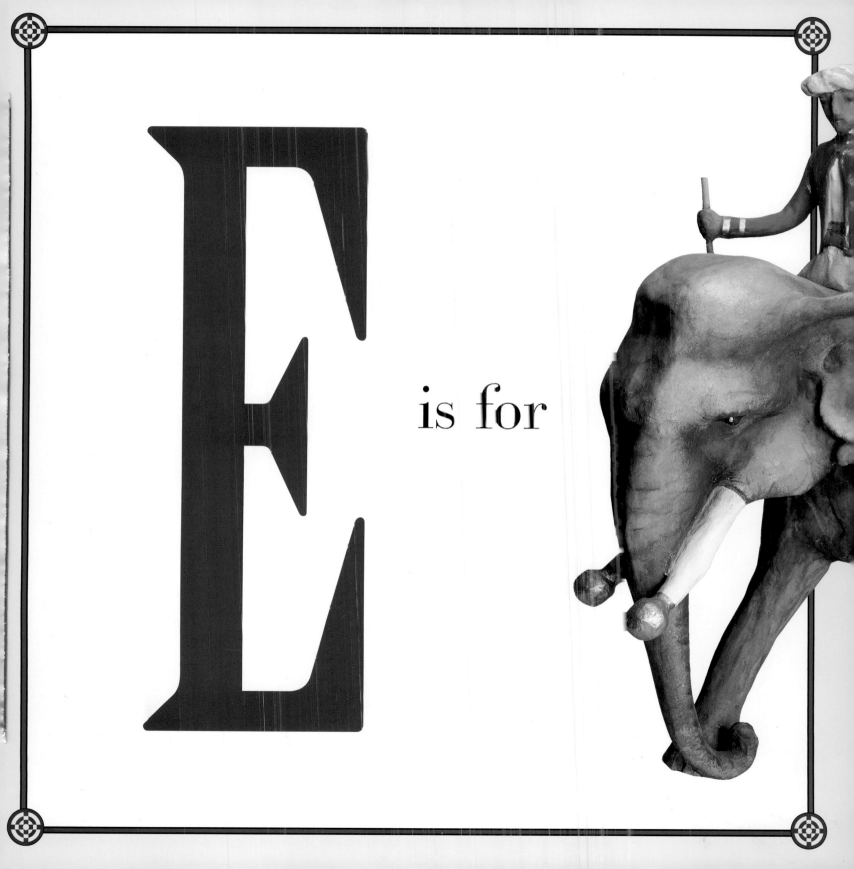

E is for

Elephant

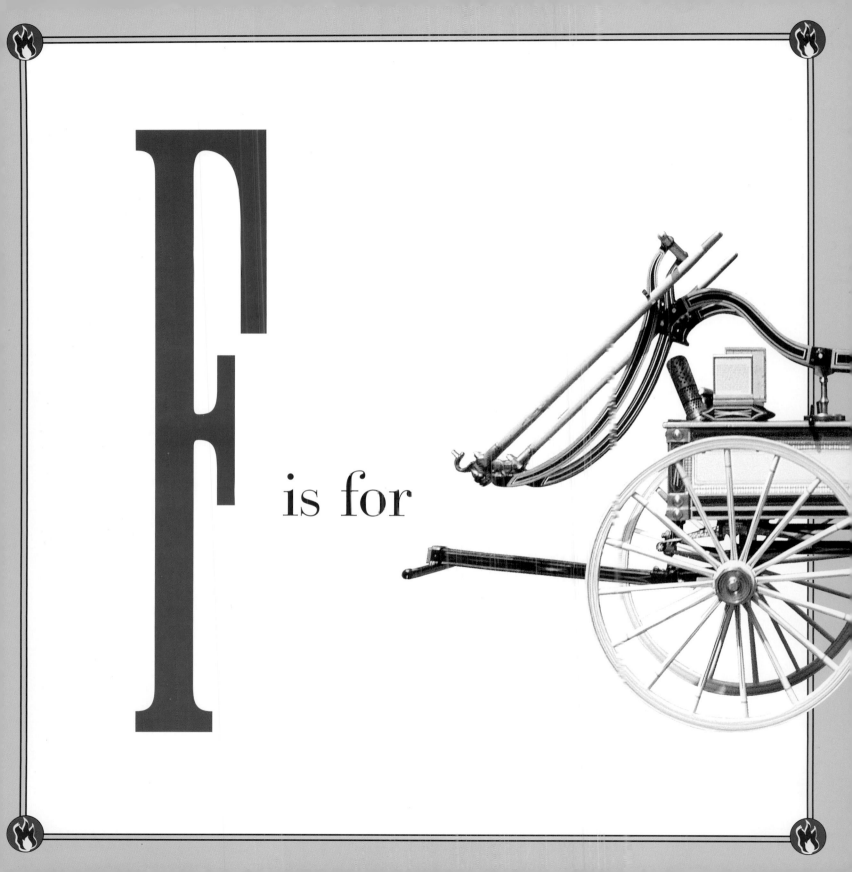

F is for

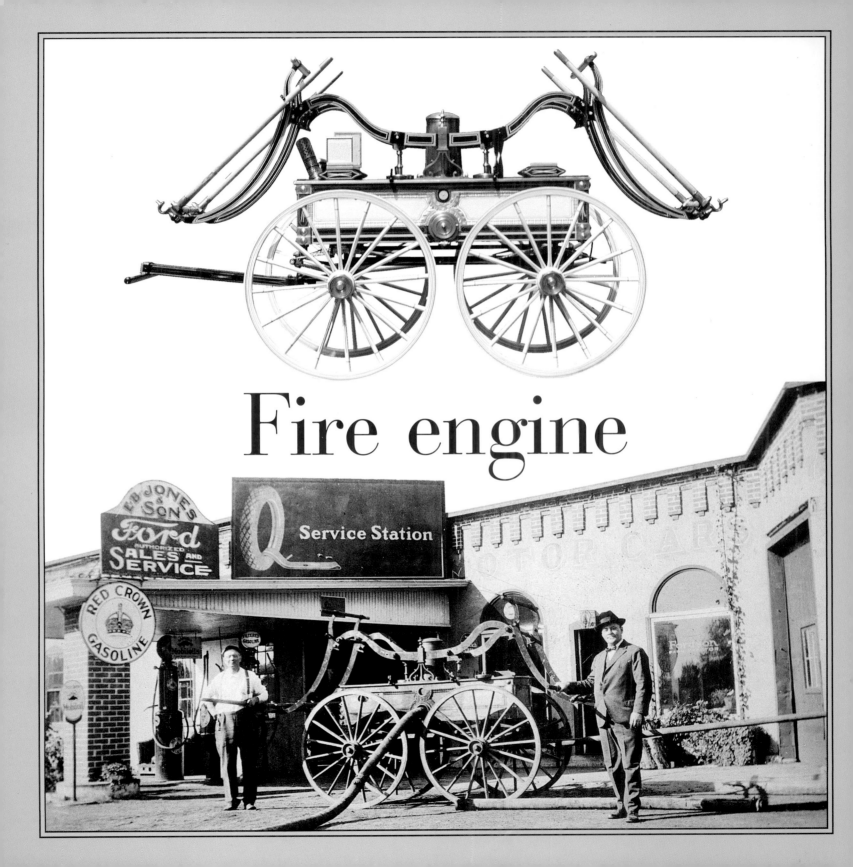

Fire engine

G

is for

Gum

H is for

Hot dog

I

is for

Ice skates

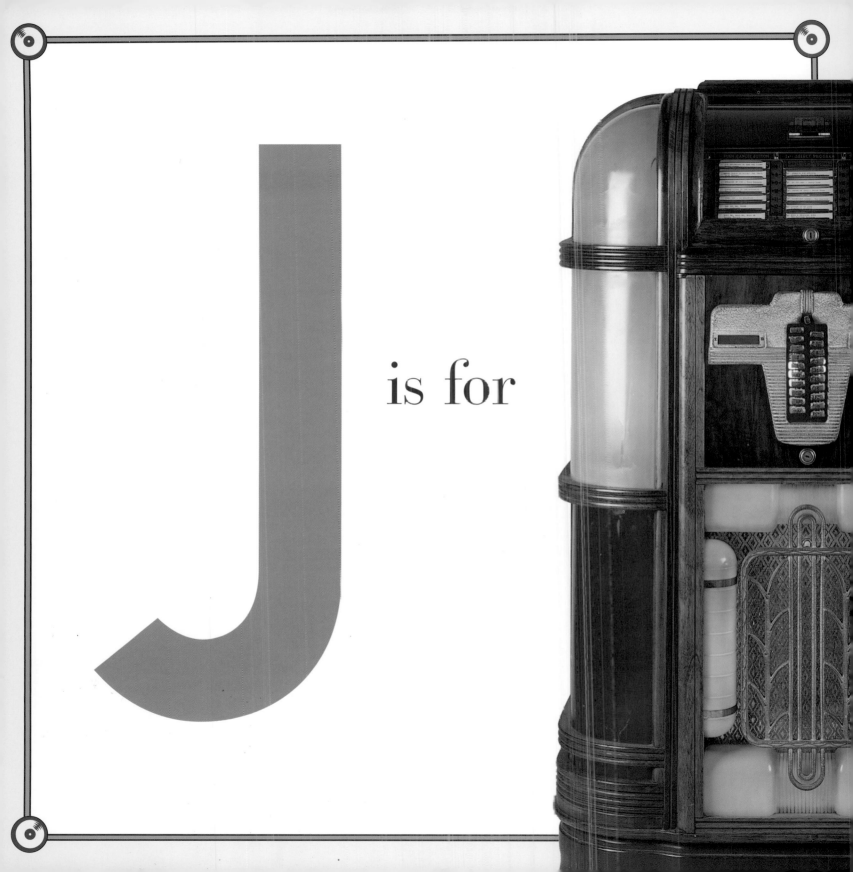

J is for

Jukebox

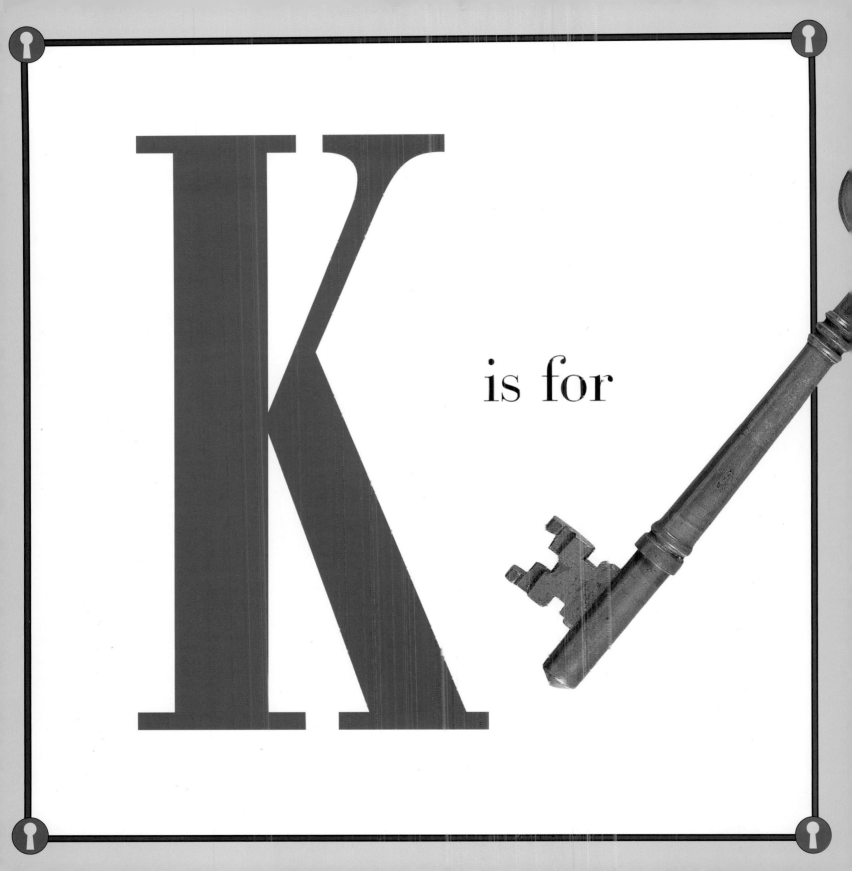

K is for

Keys

L is for

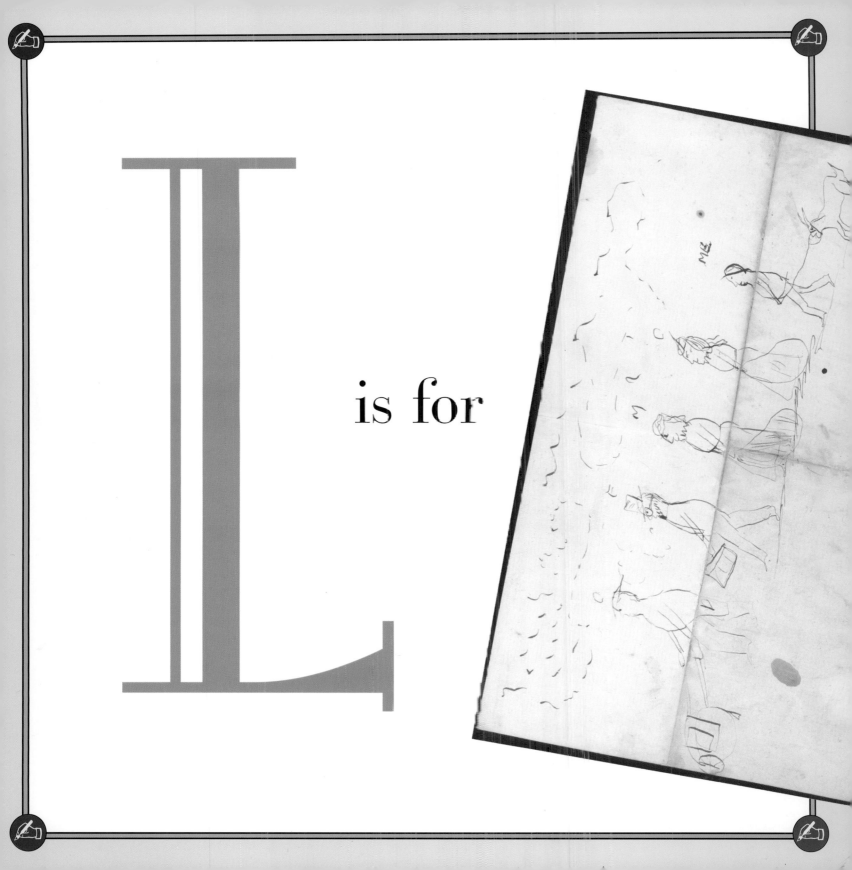

our house, I got, some
water and went out
in the yard while
my brother we...
on the roof...
for one or two...
at the end...
time we had...
we tried to...
wagon but c...
so we & put...
on a wheelb...
each of u...
a bundle a...
d for the...
park I lea...
we got a...
until the...
yard caug...
it was a...
to breath...
on fire

it out at last we
heard that there was a
little shanty that hadn't...
...ent down so we marche...
...but had to leave
...very

Lake Forest Oct 1?

Dear Chum,

We are
burnt out of house and
home and so we had
to come up here, I
suppose you would
like to hear about the
fire and how we escaped
from it. Half past one
Monday morning we
were awakened by a
loud knocking at the
front door we were
awake in an instant
and dressing ourselves
we looked about and
saw a perfect shower
of sparks flying over

Letter

M is for

Market

N is for

Chicago Daily Tribune

THE WORLD'S GREATEST NEWSPAPER

DEWEY DEFEATS

G.O.P. Sweep Indicated in State; B

REPUBLICAN TICKET AHEAD OF 1944 VOTE

Tops Coghlan in Hot Race for Attorney

RECORD CITY VOTE SEEN IN LATE TALLIES

Town Balloting Gives Trend

Newspaper

O is for

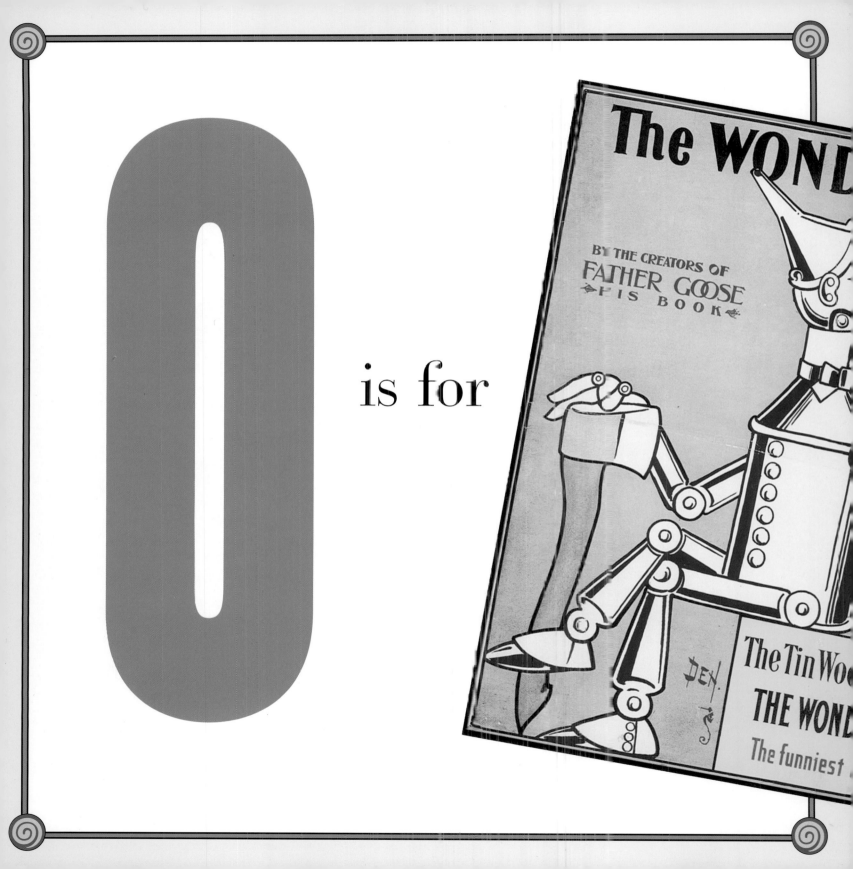

The WOND...

BY THE CREATORS OF
FATHER GOOSE
∗HIS BOOK∗

DEH.

The Tin Woo...
THE WOND...
The funniest

The Wizard of Oz

P is for

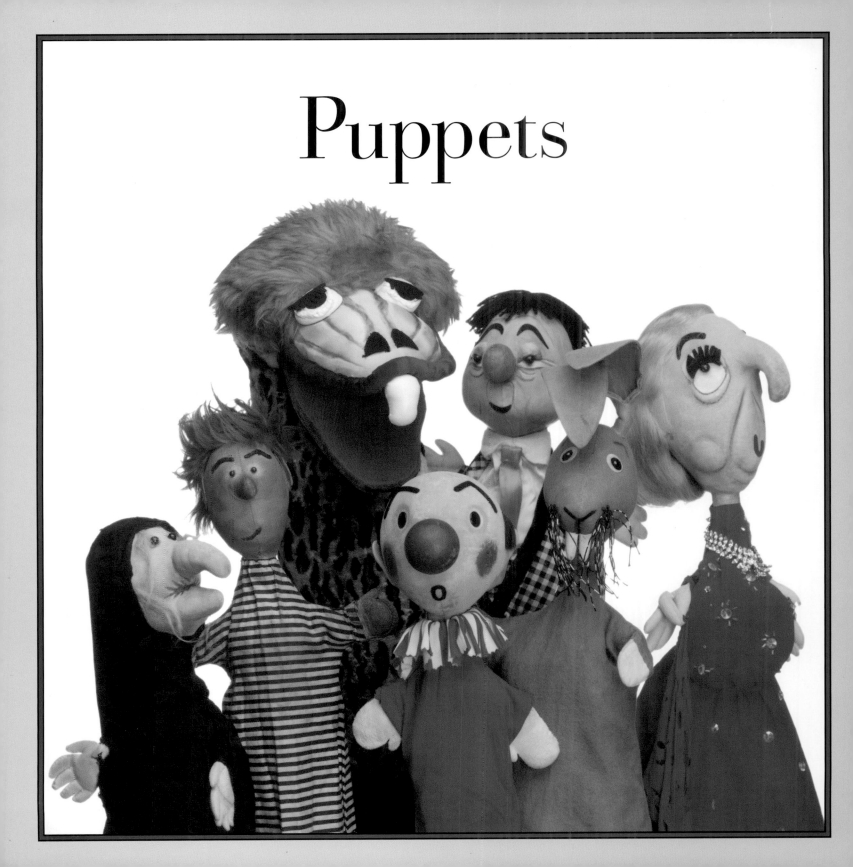

Puppets

Q is for

Quilts

R is for

Railroad

S is for

Shoes

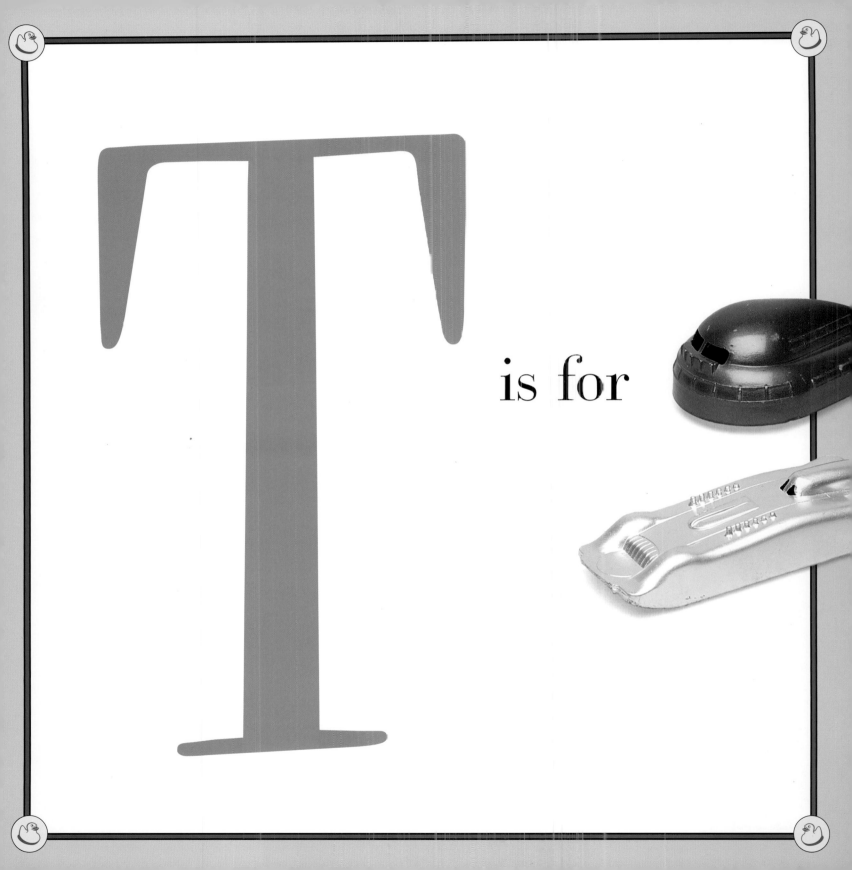

T is for

Toys

U is for

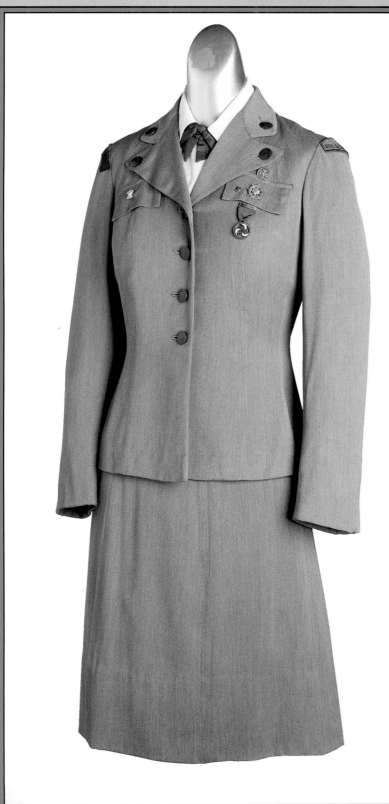

Uniform

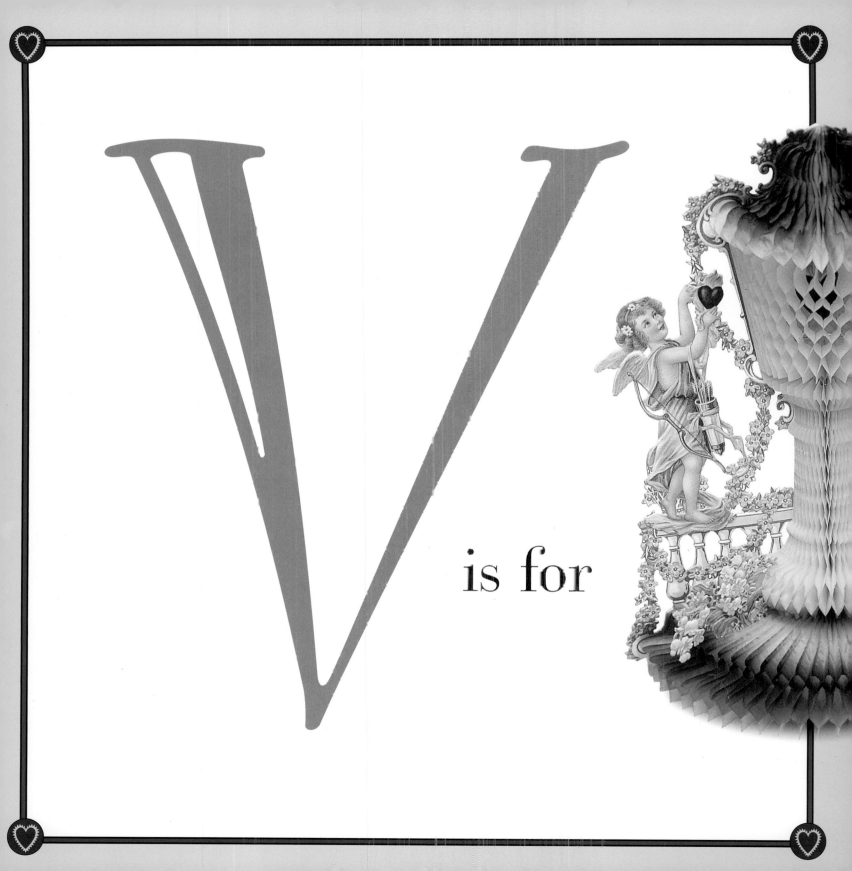

V is for

Valentines

W is for

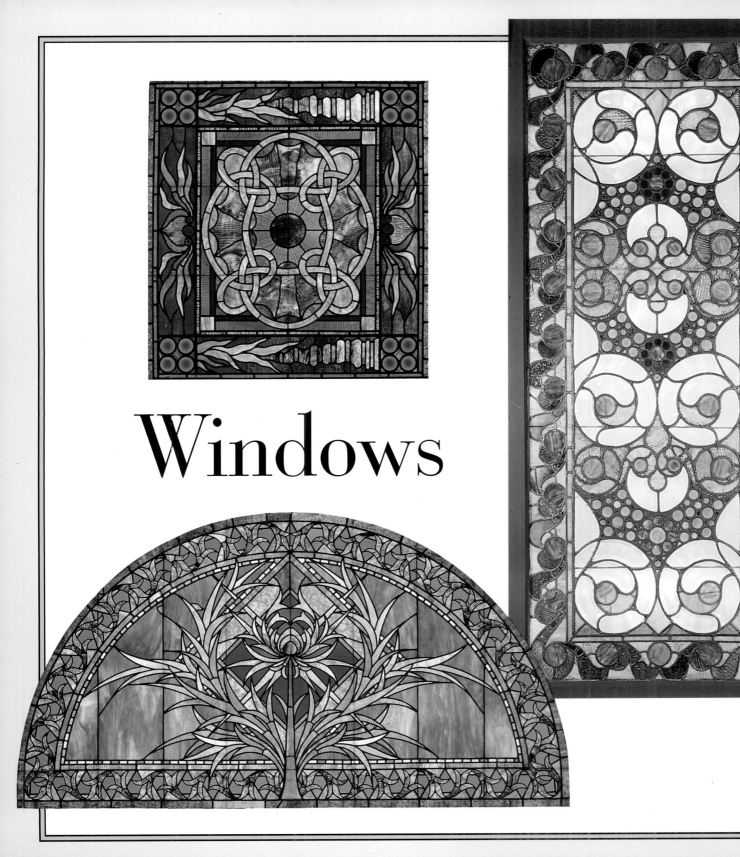

Windows

X is for

X

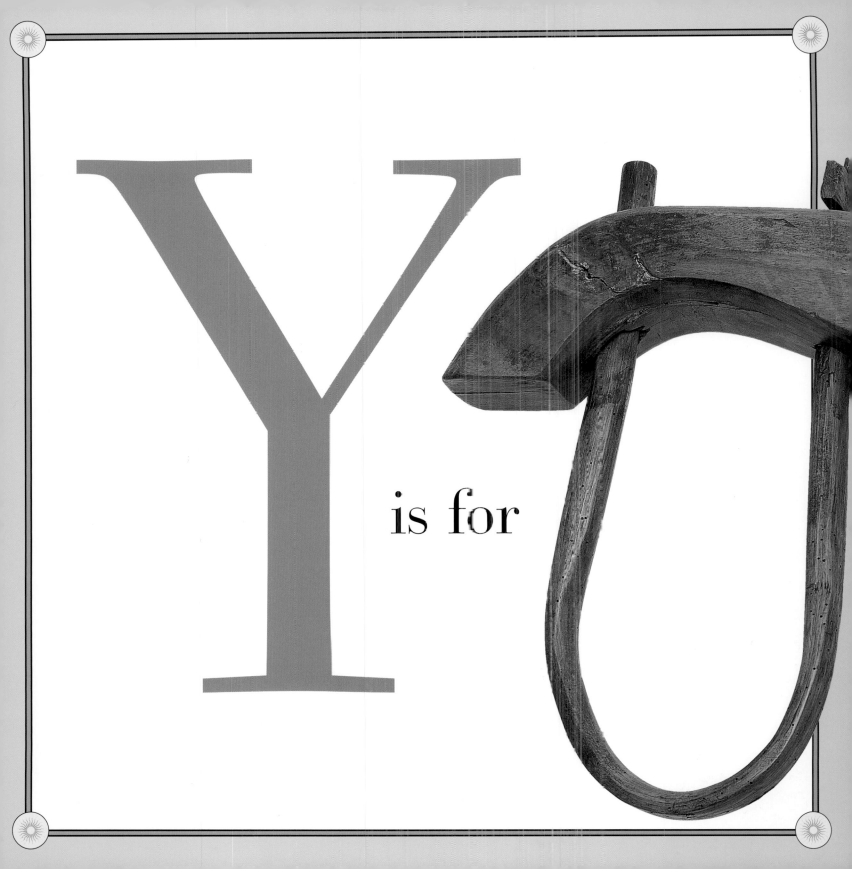

Y is for

Yoke

Z is for

Zither

A

Children have played with alphabet blocks for decades. These blocks, made by the Chicago toy company Halsam, were embossed with brightly colored pictures and letters of the alphabet. They were so popular that they could be seen in almost every American nursery by the 1950s.

B

A little girl received this pretty bicycle from her parents as a present in 1956. This rose-colored Schwinn bike, called the "Starlet," was equipped with a front light, chain-guard fender, and back rack. Engineer Ignaz Schwinn opened the Schwinn bicycle factory in 1895 on Chicago's West Side.

C

This movie camera is from Chicago's Essanay Studios, which started on Chicago's North Side in 1907. Essanay produced many early westerns before most major movie studios moved out to California. Essanay stars included cowboy Tom Mix and comedian Charlie Chaplin.

D

This doll from 1890 probably traveled to Chicago with an African American family that was migrating north. Many "folk dolls" like this one were made by local craftworkers using traditional handicraft skills and whatever materials were available in the area.

E

This elephant is advertising Hamlin's Wizard Oil. In the late 1800s, the Hamlin brothers promoted their Wizard Oil as "The Great Medical Wonder" that could cure "Rheumatism, Sprains, Bruises, Lame Back, Frost Bites, Burns, and Scalds." They even stated that the Wizard Oil could be used on horses and cattle.

F

Chicago's first fire engine, "Fire King Number One," was purchased for the city in 1835. Gurdon Hubbard bought the Fire King when a local Chicago newspaper expressed concern over the city's lack of proper firefighting equipment. Despite the addition of such equipment, much of Chicago was destroyed in the Great Fire of 1871.

G

This vending machine offers Wrigley gum, such as Doublemint or Juicy Fruit (which dates back to 1893). William Wrigley Jr. came to Chicago in 1891, and tried selling soap and baking powder. One day, he decided to offer two free packages of chewing gum with each can of baking powder. He soon realized that his customers were buying up the powder just to get the gum, and the Wrigley chewing gum dynasty was born.

H

Who doesn't love hot dogs? Oscar Mayer, a Chicago company, used toys like this "Wienermobile" to help sell its hot dogs. Chicago's meatpacking industry, and its famous stockyards, began in the mid-1800s. Huge companies such as Oscar Mayer, Armour, and Swift helped make Chicago the large city it is today.

I

These ice skates from the 1950s may seem old-fashioned, but scientists have found evidence of ice-skating that dates all the way back to 50 B.C. These skates were probably used to play hockey at a local ice rink or to skate on a neighborhood pond or lake. Humboldt Park was known for its great skating lake, while Touhy Beach was flooded to create its own ice rink.

J

A jukebox, like this one, will play your favorite record when you put money in the slot. This 1939 jukebox was called a Rockola jukebox, but not because of rock music—the name of the company president was really David Rockola.

K

As the Great Chicago Fire of 1871 spread, many people locked their doors with these big keys and ran for safety. When they returned to their houses after the fire, many discovered vacant lots where their homes had stood.

L

A little boy named Justin wrote a letter to his friend after the Great Fire of 1871. Here is what it says: "I suppose you would like to hear about the fire and how we escaped from it. Half past one on Monday morning we were awakened by a loud knocking at the front door. We were awake in an instant. We looked about and saw a perfect shower of sparks flying over our house . . . We tried to get a wagon but could not so we put two trunks on a wheelbarrow and each of us shouldered a bundle and we marched for the old skating pond, I leading my goat . . . Mother caught on fire once but we put it out."

M

Before there were grocery stores and shopping malls, people used to shop at street markets, such as the famous one on Maxwell Street. For more than 120 years Chicagoans flocked to Maxwell Street, just a mile southwest of downtown Chicago, to buy just about anything imaginable: live chickens, shoes, teakettles, used pencils, and more, at reasonable—and often negotiable—prices.

N

"Dewey Defeats Truman" is probably Chicago's most famous newspaper headline ever. The 1948 presidential race was so close that the *Chicago Tribune* declared the wrong winner, much to the delight of a gleeful Harry Truman. The *Tribune* remains one of Chicago's flagship newspapers, along with the Chicago *Sun-Times*.

O

Did you know that the famous book *The Wizard of Oz* was written in Chicago? Author L. Frank Baum wrote the Oz stories in an office in the Fine Arts Building on South Michigan Avenue.

P

These puppets, including Kukla (the little one in front) and Ollie (the dragon), had their own Chicago television show. Millions of people—adults and kids—tuned in to watch the puppets' adventures on "Kukla, Fran, and Ollie." Puppeteer Burr Tillstrom created and gave life to these charming characters, while Fran Allison served as their co-host.

Q

Quilts aren't just another kind of blanket—sometimes they can be used to tell tales. These quilts, which were made for the 1933 A Century of Progress International Exposition in Chicago, tell the story of the city, with images of Chicago's humble beginnings.

R

The Pioneer engine from 1836 was Chicago's first railroad locomotive. The railroad helped Chicago become a major city—because Chicago is in the middle of the country, everybody had to travel through it to get to where they were going.

S

Can you believe how many different types of shoes there are? Button-up boots, saddle shoes, moccasins, clogs. . . . The black shoes on the middle of the page were worn by Chicago Bulls basketball star Michael Jordan. Just below Jordan's shoes are wood pattens from the 18th century, which were worn over regular shoes to protect them from mud.

T

Many famous toys were made in Chicago, such as American Flyer model trains, Tinkertoys, Tootsietoys, and Lincoln Logs (named for Abraham Lincoln). John Lloyd Wright, son of the famous architect Frank Lloyd Wright, invented Lincoln Logs, most likely inspired by the design of his father's Imperial Hotel in Japan.

U

In 1948, when the Girl Scouts decided to update their uniforms, Chicago fashion designer Mainbocher volunteered his services. His two-piece leader suit seen here was a new addition for women who wanted a more formal uniform when representing the Girl Scouts in community activities, bringing high style to a previously ordinary outfit.

V

The custom of giving (and receiving) valentines may have begun as early as the 1400s, but commercial cards like these were not produced until the 1800s. These three dimensional cards opened for standing but folded flat for mailing. Some of these fancier valentines cost as much as ten dollars!

W

Stained glass window production has a major home in Chicago. As early as the 1850s, two Chicago stained glass window manufactories, W. S. Carse and Co. and Otto Jevne and Co., were already in business. During the building boom after the Great Fire, the city's stained glass industry exploded, resulting in windows in many different colors, shapes, and styles, as seen here.

X

The Xs on the side of the John Hancock Building are large steel beams that actually help hold up the structure. Architect Bruce Graham, who designed the Hancock, the second tallest building in Chicago, also designed the city's other famous skyscraper: The Sears Tower.

Y

This oxen yoke helped farm animals plow the fields. Before Chicago was a bustling city, it was a wide-open prairie, and early residents had to plow the land to make it ready for farming.

Z

The zither is a stringed instrument, like a banjo or a guitar, but the musician places it flat on a table and uses a special pick to play it. The German instrument is made up of a wooden box with 32 or more strings stretched across it. This zither was made by Chicagoan Theodor Zoelle around 1900.